UnHidden Reflections of the Heart

a collection of poetry

BATHSHEBA DAILEY

True Beginnings Publishing

True Beginnings logo design by Selina Ahnert

UNHIDDEN REFLECTIONS OF THE HEART

Printed in the United States of America
Printing History: First Edition, First Printing September 2012

Published by
True Beginnings Publishing

ISBN-13: 978-0615943251
ISBN-10: 061594325X

Also by Bathsheba Dailey

POETRY
Hearts and Souls Poetry Book
Soulful Writes
Soulful Writes, Part Two

Battered Shadows
with multiple authors to benefit the
National Coalition Against Domestic Violence

NON-FICTION
Five Year Old Death

COMING SOON
Scadoxus Multiflorus
Poetry under the name "Sinfully Alive"

Sinfully Becoming
Novel under the name "Sinfully Alive"

Dedication

I want to thank my girls for always having my back even at their young ages. I love you all with all of my heart. I also want to thank my mother for just being her when life is crazy. I want to thank all of my near and far away friends that have stuck by me through think and thin. A big thank you to Selina Lamken for always being just a phone call away no matter what time it is, love ya hunni. I also want to thank Blue Harvest Creative for being so great to me and helping me get my second book out again, love you all. Lastly I want to thank my hunni Mick Boice for being my strength in a time where I need it the most, I love you with all of my heart.

Un-Hidden Reflections of My Heart

An un-hidden reflection of what once was
stares back at me through the light of dawn
that can be seen from the years that have passed by,
reflections that once were un-seen.

I once followed in the footsteps of the life that was given to me,
never looking for anything more but a life full of scorn and misery.
Happiness only to come as often as the rain can be found in the desert,
my tears to be the only moistness that seeped through the ground.
A blistering pain to leave me un-sound!

I have taken path's and written my own life's story of love and heartbreak,
peace and confliction, uncertainty and self-esteem!
Sometimes I am filled with a happiness that can never be found again,
sometimes I have doubts that I will never understand, in the end my
life has been written by my own hand.

I find my inner strength that was lost to only me,
another to find it giving me
security and defining the life that was denied to me.
These are the un-hidden reflections of my heart!
A story that only I can explain of love and pain,
the dawn will guild my way!

Forever Love

I was a lost soul just existing in a world full of loneliness
and fear, nights spent writing my heart away,
days spent wishing for something more to come my way.

There you were out of the blue to take my breath away
with sweetness that at first only scared me away.
My heart had been treated so wrong, I was not looking for another
country heartbreaking song to take me away, so from you I strayed.

A lonely night, an open mind,
in you I found another heart in hiding.
I was opening up ever so slowly,
you were shut off even tighter than me I was to discover.

A text here and there, my laughter you were always after!
My heart you took into your grasp and I have never looked back.

Still fearful of what I was feeling, the thought of someone
really caring had me dazed and confused.
Sometimes I wanted to run away, making sure once again
my heart was not going to be let down
and given more unneeded pain.

I am now determined to stand strong, I know you are the love of my
life and will never treat me wrong.
My heart feels safe in your care, never to shed the first tear in despair.

In me you will find a love that will always be true to you.
Never will I let you down, you are the only man
that I will always want holding my heart in the palm of your hand.

Our lives together has just begun,
our souls knew from the beginning they had found their forever love.

Hide and Seek Words

There is not much that I fear as I have
always lived a life of a troubled mind.
Life has given me many obstacles to jump over,
here and there I will admit I wanted
nothing more but for death to take me away!
I have never really wanted
to stay in a world so full of dread and hate!

I play a song that will reach my heart
but sometimes even it will make me go farther
into a dark pit of the unknown corners that I
now have to turn, my skin burns!
My mind yearns for release; it still yet turns and turns
in life's cycle of lost memories! Maybe I should fear only me!

I try to look at the bright side,
but inside there is something missing!
I cannot put my finger on it, my mind plays havoc on me!
I am chasing to many dreams, I get restless wondering
why it is so hard to once be enough just as I am.
I dream of a death that will one day come from my own hand!

I won't feel like this for long it comes and goes,
I find a reason to put a smile on my face once again!
Just because I can hide my feelings so easily,
I make myself believe I don't need anyone but myself!
To count on anyone else would be calling my own bluff!

So I try to be fearless of the next punch that
is always to be felt in this life I have lived in called hell!
The only relief I have is in the words I so often spill,
whether they are good or bad!

My words are all that I really have;
no one can ever take them from me!
They reside in my mind like a game of hide in seek,
only by me can they ever be found!

Now that my feelings are once again written for all to read
I will light this cigarette that I really do not need
and continue on with my day.
I may even plead it to go away,
but in the end I have always been the strong one
to play in life's most treacherous games of pain!

Arms of Comfort

I lay in your arms in the comfort of your strength,
I feel safe as you pull me closer to you in your sleep.

A tingle running through my body
as you graze your fingers up and down my arm
just a loving gesture that I always find in your arms.

I get lost in your smile,
the twinkle of your eyes keeps me mesmerized.
You make me once again feel so alive, revived!

I drift to sleep with a smile on my face,
in your arms I have found the place
that I was bound to grace.

A perfect sleep I find
in the arms of the love I can no longer deny,
even in my dreams your smile is always there to find!

Confused Heart

Dazed, confused, hurt left shattered and bruised!

Depressed, weeping, hard to see through
the tears that seem to keep flowing with my hearts fears.

Lost then found,
I am so tormented and scared uncertainty I am bound!

Drifting into obliteration,
my mind is suffering with hesitation.
Day and night I cannot tell apart,
my mind sits in the dark!

Another tear to fall, another night to sleep alone.
I almost grab for my phone,
I need to hear his voice on the other end.

Nerves are strung out,
chest could burst with all of my doubts!
I try to sleep now,
wishing I knew what life is really about!

I love him with all of my being
and I just wish he could see my heart and mind
is only for him to read!

Confused

Oblivious to everything around me with my straying thoughts
I feel like I am ready to break.
My head hurts with anticipation of what more I can do.

The need to hide in a corner pausing life in its tracks
sometimes crosses my mind,
to be invisible from the world with no one to let down,
even to myself I would not be found!

In the darkness I see that my mind is playing tricks on me,
worries of things that are not needed has me down,
my heart to skip beats.

I am my own worst enemy,
fighting my own battles within myself!
I sit and watch the stars that are dimmer than normal,
I wonder if they can even feel my pain.

I look around and watch my life passing me by
and wonder when I started seeing clearer in the dark.
I have been given another chance at living life!

I no longer have to protect myself from my deceiving heart!
I no longer have to be scared into a corner to live in the dark!

Infused Hearts

Bodies entangled as pulses run high in each other's arms,
hearts infused together not making it without the other.

Spells over my mind in his presence, missing him when he is gone
leaves me feeling alone in the world.

Breathless whispers in each other's ear
as we give into each other's passionate kisses,
hands astray feeling at home.

Our love grows stronger everyday
feeling lost waiting for each other's loving grace.
Hearts playing to the sound of music,
fluttering in excitement, never to be confused!

I feel alone in a crowded room just
waiting for the time to come when he walks through my door,
once more, I feel at home.

Lips touch as they flame with love;
this is what dreams are really made of!
Never alone when together, bleakness when we are apart,
only to carry half of our heart.

Man of My Dreams

My love grows stronger everyday
for the man who has walked with me through the dark,
finding the light again as I walk farther from my past pains.

I entrust my hand into his,
he leads me into the world that has much to offer us.
With him I now feel nothing but positive energies
from the life I am now to live.

I was walking life like a blind person
falling into the shadows of my past demons.
I was so sure life had nothing left for me
but miseries to relive every day.

Nightmares woke me out of my already restless sleep,
all of that changed with our long awaited meeting.
Now dreams of kisses under the moonlight
in his arms are what I see,
my heart has been completely taken by the man of my dreams.

I now thank the lord for unanswered prayers!
I now see his plan for me!
In your arms is where I have always meant to be,
warm and safe from the world
that I always believed was out to get me.

I take my heart and hand it to him in hopes that this time
I will not find any more miseries!
With him I believe my heart is finally safe!
I need to no longer look for my great escape!
My life has been laid down in front of me
and in its plans I want to be.

The Perfect Ending

Your heart has taken a grasp of mine,
I cannot hold these feelings in any longer.
Your arms around me makes my mind wander
into far off places, our lives spent together
for the rest of what remains.

I feel free, I feel relief,
I have finally found the man that was molded just for me.
Tender embraces, a kiss to your loving face,
in your arms I feel my safest.

My nightmares have been replaced by sweet dreams of lullabies,
fears gone now of old memories,
only dreams of the rest of my life being spent
with the man who holds the other half of me can I see.
Is it fate? Was this meant to be?

Had we suffered heartaches from so many others
so we would have the pleasure to meet?
Was our lives already written in the moon and stars,
did they lead you to me?

I almost missed my chance,
it makes me shudder to think of you not being here with me.
My courage finally took hold
and I meant the man whole truly make me feel whole.
My fright was spell bound on my previous life,
never had I been treated right.

I finally opened my eyes and listened to your words,
from then on out I knew this love was one worth the fight,
my heart now being treated right!

I hear our story in the love songs that play on the radio!
My heart beats to the tune of yours!
Our souls intertwined, dancing to a lost memory,
worlds apart they finally see they had found the one
they so often had seeked.

We have just begun to live our lives
the way that we had dreamed of for so long.
The perfect beginning to a happy ending!

Childhood Beliefs

As a child I expressed my feelings through paper and pen,
the world has changed so much
it is now a keyboard and screen to entertain me.

As a child I believed in fairy tales,
the beautiful girl being rescued by the dashing prince on a steed.

Now that I am a woman I see things for what they really are,
men come also with hearts not just amour,
some need saved in return, their souls to yearn!

As a child I could not wait for the summer's rain,
so many puddles to find and prance in,
shoes to dry when it was time to go in.

I still wait for that summer's rain as an adult,
not to prance in puddles,
but to dance as the world is cleaned again
from the rain that is pouring down on me.

Childhood dreams and wonderment's to change
as the time passes me slowly by,
as an adult I see the world through grown up eyes!

Beauty and pain, tears in the rain,
dashing princes that need their own fairy tale come true,
through the eyes of a woman my mind has been renewed.

Bleeding Tears

Tear soaked pillows with endless grief,
solitude like no one could ever believe.

A heart to be shattered once again,
no one wants this child in pain!
Left alone wondering who to blame.

Holidays hold no joys at all for them,
all they see is more lonesome friends.
Homeless, parent less and hopelessly alone.

A child on her own searching for answers she will never find.
Parents gone away with a life she was not permitted to be a part of.

Tears of love, tears of sadness,
tears she feels bleeding every night on her pillows.
Sheets she alone will change when morning comes,
out the door her dreams once again runs.

Give her hope, give her joy, let's just for once fill her void.
A cup of tea, a bite of bread, a dry pillow to lay her head.

A single word to fill her heart,
a single line to give her hope,
a single poem to give her meaning,
a single book can mean tonight she will be eating!

Hearts Afire

I turned away,
not even thinking of giving it a chance!
Never again would I be hurt by any man,
no way would I give another a chance.

Slowly giving in, just watching him!
I couldn't help but laugh at what I seen,
he seemed down to earth and I wondered
if this was really him, was he maybe different?

A comment here and a text there,
a visit from him and I knew my heart was
taken from him so easily.
Arms I never will want to leave,
a heart that I will always dream of belonging to me.

We swore we were only going to be friends,
our hearts were always hurt
until even they could no longer bend.
A few dates and it was all over, our love for each other
broke down our walls and took over.

A life full of dreams is on our horizon,
in each other's arms our true love has finally risen.
Life so full of each other's loving embraces,
another kiss from him takes my breath away.
With him my heart is no longer a stray!

Remembering Long Days Ago

A lonely thought creeps into my mind of days long ago when life
should of been of fairy tales and families love.

Thrown out to the gutter,
a mother who was nothing more than a monster on the inside.
Never caring for the ones she had brought into the world,
her own happiness and men were all she looked forward to.

A dad we never really seen,
only in our minds did we have long ago memories.
Lost to us from a very young age,
sometimes it is hard to turn that page.

Family we really never knew,
her life was always to change, everyone else to blame.
The same old story we would hear,
as we watched her cry into her beer.

Move away to a faraway place, now our lives would really change.
Giving her chances she did not deserve,
not one of her men were anything other than a pervert.

She made her choice and threw us away,
never again would we see her face,
she is nothing to me now but a childless mother, what a disgrace!

Never will she see her grandchildren,
this is what she had wanted from the beginning,
a life of nothing more but her endless parting.

Many roads have been traveled since childhood;
many things will never be understood.
I have forgiven her now that I am older,
I pity her more than I hate her.

She is nothing to me now but a bad memory,
but yet sometimes I cannot help but wonder where she could be.
I think of her in our younger days,
when she was the mother we all praised.

She lost her will and lost her love,
she lost the person we both so cherished and loved.
She has left my mind for the most part,
but sometimes I can still feel her in my heart.

I may not talk about her much
but as her child I miss her once motherly touch.
She may be dead or even alive;
once again I shut her out of my mind!

My Babies

I love the way you look so fresh in the morning,
even when you are crying and moaning
wanting just another minute in bed.

I love your sweet little smiles,
I can see irony all over your face;
I start to look for a broken vase.

I love the way your eyes get real wide,
the story you are telling you explain was wild, at least to a child.

I love the way you get real excited,
your room is now spotless and you want to prove it.

I love the way your eyes switch in your sleep,
smiling at whatever it is you are dreaming.

I love you from here to the moon,
I am dreading the day that my baby girls are grown.

You will always be sweet and perfect to me,
always my baby girls no matter what your age may be.

Words

My mind is crazed,
not even I can think of a word to say!
I look around and even listen to a song,
but the words are so bundled up they all sound wrong.

My mind had grown weary, my heart is so full
it just wants to spend every second and word on him!
I still see my dreams,
but now they are more of him and me.

Five girls who needs the best,
my words for now will need to rest!
I will be back for this I am sure,
but right now my life's happiness rest
in my family's arms more.

A poet's words will never go away,
but life can be gone tomorrow or even today!
I may back up just a little bit,
but be assured you will always see the words I have written.

I am following my heart in so many poems I have written,
it is time I once again start to live them!

Perfect Pair

I walk in his shadow that gives me the strength
I need to make it through
my days that can seem so hard and full of struggles.

He gives me the willpower I need to see life for what it really is
when I would rather turn a blind eye
to never see what the world can really hold for me.

A sweetness in his stroking touch
as his fingers play silently on my flesh,
a soft word in my ear he puts.

Roaming lips so softy to my cheek that
it sometimes cannot be felt,
the meaning of true love and compassion,
in his arms I melt.

In his eyes I can see the love
I had always wanted to be in!
In his heart I can see me! In his mind I want to be!
A life full of happiness I live in now,
his love I will always find my strength in.

My real love has finally been sent to me!
He is the only one I see in my dreams when I can finally sleep.
Another kiss from his lips,
sends me into an endless bliss of passionate love.

We fit each other like the perfect pair,
in his shadow I will never feel despair.

Speaking Hearts

I could only dream of such sweet embraces
as the tears still silently fall invisibly down my reddened cheeks,
my life just a moment seemed so right
and now we once again lean towards things that will never change,
our past we can never erase!
But with each other we can find so many more brighter days.

He leans in toward me
as I silently pray for his eyes to speak a million okays,
telling me in there beauty that life will finally start with today.
The past can be erased! His lips softly touch mine
as we feel our life's reflections shatter in each other's loving faces,
the mirror we had hid behind nothing more
now than shattered glass that we wish never again to find.

Our true love we can finally see, our souls lingering together
so high the heavens we can almost reach.
Bodies intertwined for the rest of our lives!
My future can be seen in the pools of his eyes!
Our lives no longer lived behind disguises,
our hearts sweet melody can be heard miles away
in our dance of love making.

Juke Box

We all have been down that same lonely road,
love gone bad and hearts that have grown cold.

Like a country song playing on the juke box
in the back of a dark bar, finding peace in the drink
that you sip through a straw!

You know this song,
you have heard it many times before,
grab another drink as your tears once again start to pour.

A shadow finds its way to your lonesome place
that you have hidden yourself in, tonight you look for sin.

A dance among strangers, a giggle in their ear,
another drink to chase away the rest of your lingering fears.

A pocket full of change,
in the juke box it is to go to waste.
Another dance before you leave the bar,
you can only wish for no tomorrow.

In a strangers arms tonight you may lay,
tomorrow you will once again remember all of your heartaches.
In borrowed time you have once again made another mistake!

Gripping arms to hold you for now tightly,
chasing away the guilt you know you will later feel.
That country song you are still to hear,
you reach for yet another beer.
Crying your tears!

Ticking Clock

To my mother and father,
I know sometimes I get busy in life
and you think you are just a bother between house and kids,
work and words that need to be written
I may sometimes forget the clock is ticking.

My life has me on a whirlwind
spinning and my mind can sometimes forget
the pair who gave me this life to live.
I love you so and just wanted you to know
that my heart is never too far away from you both.

If you give just one more minute, just another second,
I will pick up the phone that I have lately forgotten!
Until I do just remember this,
I am still your little girl and that I could never forget!

Breathe

Breathe in the fresh morning's air,
the day may not be all that you seem to wish for.

Think of home when you get all bent out of shape,
your lover's smile is your greatest escape.

Feel your heart race, think of a better place, your children's faces!
A love no greater, never a minute wasted!

Listen to their childhood wonders,
at night watch their eyes as they slumber.

Never a minute to waste!
They grow up an adult to take their place,
you wish once again for these days.

Watch the wind as it softly blows!
The seasons change, our days are numbered
so make them count today!

Live life to the fullest!
Let no one take away the happiness you wish to feel!
The ones who wish for your tears are
not worth your presence any longer,
they are only time wasted!

Breathe in the fresh morning's air,
your love and children being your everything in life,
think only of the ones who treat you right.

Give thought to your day,
for tomorrow it may all go away, in this life we play!

A New Beginning

Arms and bodies entangled together, the feel of him
driving my senses wild with anticipation and wanting.
A love that flies above all else, my heart is now selfish for his love.

My heart has meant its match,
a love that I will fight for and never let go of from here on out.
Tender words of endearment that I have never heard before,
coming from the sweetness of my lovers embrace.

My life has brought on more meaning,
with him I only search for a better me!
My heart is the one I always want him to see,
my heart finally released belonging to him only, finally at peace!

Never have I ever felt so loved,
never could I of dreamed there was such an angelic man
treading this life I have always felt so lost in,
it took his words of encouragement to finally see

I am worth more than what I have ever been given.
In his love life is now worth really living,
in his arms I feel a new life beginning.

A new beginning is better than an old ending;
with him I can see so many dreams coming true!
It took a real man to make me see,
I am worth something so much more, just by being me!

A Left Alone Child

Why do you let that child in your home?
She has taught your own so much wrong!
That is why she has been left alone.

Why do you risk this theft in the night?
She deserves nothing in life!
That is why she has been left alone!

Don't let her in, run her off, she is too full of sin.
She cannot be helped!
That is why she has been left alone!

Look at her father, look at her mother!
and have you ever meant any of her sinful brothers?
That is why she has been left alone!

She deserves to be no more than what she has been given;
her life was in the stars already written!
That is why she has been left alone!

Why do I let her in my home?
Why do I feed the child who does not even have a crumb?
Why do I tell her I love her?
Just as much as my own?
Why do I risk losing everything that I own?

Because she was left alone! I have been in her footsteps,
I was left alone!
I never knew what love was until fourteen years old,
which is why I will not leave her alone!

That is what love really means,
that is what I learned when I was seen,
for the child that had always been left alone
only dream of what love could be, if felt for me!

Why does she walk through my door at all hours of a night?
Why do I feed a child who has never been treated right?
She was left alone, with no real home!

All of God's Children

I think of God and what his plans are for us,
I do not cross the threshold
like I did years ago
but our savior is always in my heart where he belongs.

I look around me at people running around
believing they are better than those
who read their bible only at home,
I wonder then where they are
when so many children go
without so much as even any kind of hope.

No love, no true home, just the streets to roam.
Crying out for help, turned away without
so much as a second glance.
They beg for love, something so easily to give!
They are not even worth any of this,
what God preached so powerfully for us to give!

Call them bad, they are just sad!
Tell them they are not any good, they just want to be understood!
Turn your backs on them, they are driven to sin!
Turn your eyes from them and pretend you do not see,
they are stealing and begging because they just want to eat!

We will now turn our backs on the children God so loved!
Because they are not any longer
worth the blood his son spilled for us!
We will let them wander on the streets begging to eat
and a warm place to sleep as we talk about their bad seed!
Because we are to blind to see,
they are dependent only on you on me!

Dreams to Come True

You are all that I have ever dreamed,
I have been looking for the perfect one
to fit me for so very long I had almost given up.
And there you were!

I was blinded at first,
my fear of feeling anything was holding me forever back!
I opened my eyes and this I will never regret!

My pulse runs high on the mere thought of you taking me in your
arms, holding me tenderly from harm.
A tear is falling from my eyes,
just these words to you makes me feel so very alive.

A dream to come true when the world felt like there was nothing left
for me but lonesomeness and a heart full of wishes.
The emptiness I had felt has finally been
pleasantly filled with your sweet loving kisses.

No one could ever take your place!
Your smile and face are all I want to see,
your arms are all that I want and need to feel alive and really me.

My dreams have finally come true!
My heart, mind and body only belongs to you!!

A Perfect Fit

My eyes are opened to a perfect love affair,
life seemed to elude me before,
leaving me in wonderment of happy couples
walking hand in hand.
You could feel their love in the air!
A perfect fit!

A smile has crept on my face that
has not been erased for so long now;
he makes me feel like I am a part of him.
A perfect fit!

My heart pitter patters at the mere thought of him,
knowing I am the one he wants to love
and share his life's dreams with.
A perfect fit!

He creeps into my sleep of a night,
my nightmares have finally taken a flight
where it belongs, in the past to shallowly fall.
A perfect fit!

Life has opened a door that has forever been closed in my face,
our love will become stronger throughout all of our days.
His face is all that I see,
forever loving him and all that he has shown me.
A perfect fit!

A perfect fit of hearts and minds,
not everything needs to be agreed upon.
Love is in the air,
my life no longer one of despair and tears,
no longer filled with endless fears.
A perfect fit!

One and Only Me
(Help to stop bulling in your schools)

I walk these halls feeling the eyes on me,
here they come again ready to tease.

My grades get made fun of,
I am too smart to be a part of the crowd.
No one wants me around!

My smile reaches my eyes,
why is it that my weight is all that they can see?
The real me not found!

I go to church because I love my lord,
he is the one who let me join the world.
I get made fun of though for being a Christian girl!

I wonder why we all cannot just get along,
it seems like even the adults are bullies and try to hurt the small.

From a child's eyes all that I can see is torment and misery.

Wars to take place,
another's heart to break.
Another life at stake!

I will go to school now and be the best that I can be
and hope this time you will look at me
with your heart and not what you want your eyes to see.

I can only be myself and that is all that I can be!
If you give me a chance
you will see that I am the perfect mold of me!

I Miss the Good Ol Days

There's not much I can really say
about the music we hear on the radio today.
I am a country girl all the way,
but even the new Hank has lost his way.

I want to hear about the love of younger days,
Johnny and June made us laugh when they sang time's a wasting,
she sure did make him walk the line.

Patsy Cline and Loretta Lynn everyone thought
they hated each other but they were the best of friends
singing their pure country hearts away,
nothing like these girls today.

I can remember when Garth loved to sing,
but that was before Trisha stole him away,
at home he twiddles his thumbs
looking at his guitar he is no longer allowed to play.
What a shameless waste!

Paycheck playing old violin still gets me today,
his words fall true for so many that sits in depression every day.

Fancy was one of my favorites,
I miss the Reba who sang of true heartbreak
and not of all the mistakes that women make.

I miss all of the true country stars who have now stood
aside to let a bunch of fakes take their places,
country music is doomed and will never be the same.

A Lover's Lullaby

Hold me in your arms and never let me go,
turn the music on and dance with me pulled real close.
Your chin to lay on the top of my head
as my face is nestled into your chest.

Our hearts beating in the perfect rhythm,
the song we listen to leaving our minds wide open.
Dance with me just a little bit closer,
let me feel the words that are being spoken.

A tender look up at your face,
reminds me why I wanted to dance in your embrace.
The song fades away into the night,
but we still dance to the words that fit us so right.

A lover's lullaby!

Imperfectly Perfect

We are imperfect for each other!
We really are nothing alike at all
but his arms are all I want to feel around me
until the mornings dawn.

He can watch television as I listen to the country music,
his face though is the one I will see in the words
of that beautiful love song.

He can drive his big truck on full blast and
I cannot drive a lick at all
but his lips are the best that I have ever felt.

We are not alike at all,
if you think about it we are imperfect together by far,
but he is the holder of my heart.
I never thought I would find this in my lifetime,
but happiness is now truly mine.

We are imperfectly perfect together!

Unseen Dreams

Soul mates broken and torn to shreds,
his weakness has finally given in.

He was not strong enough to fulfill his needs,
he ran scared from the unseen.

He wishes he had been a man of younger age,
not so use to his now quieter days.

He had yearned for her over so many years,
his heart though could not handle all of his fears.

He will spend the rest of his life thinking about what could of been,
now to realize he had even lost his very best friend.

He can live his life as a fake,
now to drink away all of his pain.
She can never give him what he needs,
even her heart is useless in his dreams.

He watches as his soul mate finds another,
the only thing to give him peace is knowing it is
only her heart that she is letting go.

They will meet in the heavens above,
as their souls finally find the one that they were made for.

He tries to deny this to himself,
but yet his mind is always searching her out!
He once again tries to close his eyes,
this is where he sees her in a new life.

He wakens to take another drink,
this time he will make sure he is too tired to even dream!

Tick Tock, Writer's Block

Tick tock I watch the clock,
I am so tired but yet my mind won't stop!
What do I want to say that has not been
written already on paper by my pen?

Here I go again my mind to spin,
it is turning like a dryer on full speed,
I am so drained and my body is weak!

My head hurts like it never has before,
those words I want are somewhere stuck
behind a tightly closed off door.

My heart is racing as fast as my mind,
there are so many words that I wish to find.

Give me a subject of your choice,
I can write about it the best that I can,
but yet it will not stop
the words that has yet to be found.

I am tired and I am weak,
give me those words that I seek!
o I can finally rest in peace!

Tick tock she looks at the clock!
She just may finally have writer's block!

Morning Sun

She looks out her window as the sun gently touches the sky, the moon has started to drift away and it is harder now to see, behind the tress it now hides.

The leaves have left long ago, now only to be touched with spots of snow that are melting away turning to water as it drops to the ground. She hears a songbird sign her good morning, at least she can believe he is doing so, warming her soul, touching her heart, believing in this moment the world is only hers to cherish and she relishes that thought for right now, the world is hers she will shout to the top of her lungs.

She will tell the world that her dreams will come true, no one will knock them to the ground, I will pick them back up and tread on until they are all found!! You cannot tell me they are hopeless silly dreams, they keep me going when life is nothing more but broken hearts that keep you locked behind steel doors, crying on your wooden cold floors!

These are my dreams, they are not yours to decide when I should give them up and throw them away, my life is not one of play, I have faith that you will believe in me one day. She calms now after her yelling has subsided, a weight has been lifted off of her chest, a smile comes to her face as she wonders… (Had anyone listened? Had anyone heard? Do they now believe in her?)

She walks now from her window, the sun has now set in its cozy spot for the day. The song bird is gone now, he has flown to another window, if you listen you will hear him sing a song to you, he is waiting for you to tell him your story now. Scream to the top of your lungs, get it out and into the open, this is your life and it will not leave you broken!! Believe in yourself, because let's face it world, if we don't know one else will!

Hearts at Home

The softness of his voice
telling me endearing things in my ear
leaves me with a shiver coursing down
my already weakened spine.

A touch to my face
as I look into his eyes
makes me say thank you lord
for so many nights spent alone to cry.

His words of toughness
trying to make me not see,
what is hidden within him buried deep.
He is as scared as me, we had given into defeat.

His fingers intertwine mine
sending warmth through my body,
never had I felt so secure in just being me,
for anyone to see.

I sit patently waiting for it all to blow up in my face,
but he comes back to me,
always to put a true smile where
so many tears had left their traces.

My heart races at the thought of his arms
holding me so tightly, his face is what I see
when my mind finally lets me sleep,
only of him do I dream.

The feelings I have had to hold on to
for so very long has finally found
the one who I can love,
making my heart feel at home, no longer alone.

In a Man's Thoughts

He sits alone in his own thoughts of long ago
days when he could love with his whole heart
and never worry about the cost of another heartache.

His mind is tantalized of finding the right one
who can fit in the crook of his arm
to love and fill him with warmth and trust.

He tries to hide away and act like he needs no one,
hiding the fact that his life has so many times
been left also in heartbreaking turmoil.

He is a man who has given up the thought of finding
anything more than what he believes he deserves,
he believes his chances has faded away
like the candle that slowly loses its flare.

He sits in a room day dreaming to himself,
is this the way his life will forever be,
keeping his heart upon an un-noticed shelf.

His mind wanders as he drifts to sleep,
will he ever find the one that he sees in his dreams.

Uncovered

There are words I want to say
but my heart keeps them all locked up tight and at bay.

There are dreams I want to live
but I cannot let myself once again be hurt, never to forgive!

There are thoughts I want to share
but my mind won't let me crack them open like an peanut shell,
left unprotected and bare.

There are boulders I want to move,
but if I do will there be any use?

There are things in life I want to find,
but my heart is closed off by these walls
that seem too high to climb.

There are so many things that may never be found by me,
my life being one that not even I wish to seek.

There are mysteries in life that we all want to un-cover,
these are the things that will always leave us alone to cower.

I Feel You

I can feel him watching me through the window of the screen.
My heart cries out still at times for the one
who tricked me into believing.

I have taken a vow to move on with my life,
But I will always miss the words that to my ears sounded right.

I can feel his heart still today,
it is crying out begging me to forgive him for all of my pain,
mine to do the same.

We could not make it work,
but we will always be the best friends that only we could be.
No one to really know the secrets that we will always keep.

You are always in my heart and you
will be there until the world finally tears are bond apart.
I am sorry for all of your pain, I no longer blame.

I forgive what you reeked down on me,
I know in your heart you are sorry just like me.

Live happily and dream your dreams, you deserve nothing less
than to achieve everything that you were meant to be.

Gun Shy

I am gun shy and scared every day that I wake up,
I just know any minute
something will blow up in my face.

I have cried a thousand un-seen tears,
whispered a million un-heard prayers.
My life has never been the kind that you would want to live,
most would have ran and hid.

A childhood of dread and wishing life would take me now,
to adulthood of pain and many doubts.

I am gun shy from everyone I meet, trusting anyone
has never served me well, I think of all of this and dwell.

My mind is haunted by so many memories that
I wish I could erase with ease,
but still I sit here helplessly, blinded by my haunting dreams.

I want to move on and forget the pain,
enjoy the one who has once again put a smile on my face.

I am gun shy and my shield is still up,
I just want to once again learn to love and trust.

I will take it one step at a time and hope
I am not once again left behind.
I will lower the shield one day soon I hope
and forget about the ones who left me
shattered and broke.

Redefined

My life has been redefined
by the arms of a man that feels the same as I.
His words drip with honey as they speak words of a better life.

I listen in anticipation to the next thing that
may fall from his sweet lips.
I have seen just a very small part of his heart,
just a glimpse of a brand new start.

My body tingles with an energy that screams out his name,
with him I feel no pain.
My heart is being rebuilt to perfection
and it will never feel the same.

My mind wanders again to dreams that were let go,
never did I believe my love would once again show,
never to be at peace I believed.

I walk in the shadow of a greater life,
one that I know I will never have to hide.
I feel my pulse quicken when I think of him,
my dreams are more now than long ago memories.

One brick at a time is being left behind,
our story is left to unfold in the arms
of a lover touch that will never grow old.

Forgiven

He will never see what is right in front of his eyes
but that is fine, he can keep denying
because I can finally see and I am fine
without him or his deceiving.

I have found what I was not at all looking for,
my heart now an open door.
His memory still plays on my mind once in a great while
but I can finally feel free and smile happily.

There are times like right now
that I wonder if I was really ever there
or was my heart, a replacement, like a spare.
Seems so unfair!

I listen again to songs that touch my heart,
a certain one means so much more.
Unanswered prayers repeats it's tune in my mind,
maybe now I will see he was never meant for me.

I will love him until the day that I die,
but as a memory that I loved even if his words
were nothing more than lies.

I can go now in a brisk step away from him
and may even cry a tear or two,
but my heart can no longer feel alone,
my mind now no longer will go back to him and roam.

I will always be grateful to him,
he showed me a life I had so long ago forgotten,
to love with all of me,
and that will forever be in my mind his graceful memory.

Tick Tock

A shadow is watching from the wall, tick tock a grandfather clock yells. You give a searching look with fear in your heart trying to figure out the image through the dark.

You hear a whisper that is so low you think you have imagined it for just a second before it is heard just a little bit louder the second time.

Your skin crawls as you start to feel tears falling from your eyes, praying you could figure out the voice that is being disguised.

You slowly stand up and get the courage to walk toward the shadow that has been playing with your mind, it has disappeared out of your sight and within just moments you finally realize, it was your guardian angel just stopping by to tell you hi.

You lie back down and slowly drift to sleep, for the first time ever you begin to believe there is more to the eyes than what you will ever see! Calmness takes a hold of you as you finally fall in a peaceful slumber, in the morning your mind is left to wonder....

A Brighter Light Than Day

Forbidden treasuries hidden in the stars,
the moon is so bright
it is hard to tell them apart.

A glistening light sparkles its power for me to see.
Such a small light to be so full of life
and inspiring dreams to be.

I hold my camera in my hand
just waiting for the right time to take
a snap shot of the sky so full of demands,
a beautiful sight to my eyes.

I lean back on a tree and just watch
the shapes that take place, before my eyes
they seem to always be changing with such grace.

A tear trickles down my face as I imagine
what really occurs among the stars and moon,
such a beauty to behold,
a thousand stories have been told
under the nights sky that seems so entrancingly bold.

I never took the picture that I sought out to take,
but in my mind the beauty
of that night will forever be engraved!

The star and the moon are to be
the only ones to know what I prayed.

Chest Full of Notes

She sits in her living room looking out into space remembering so much that the time had seemed to erase. A lost love plays on her mind frequently as she tries to remember his face, every last crease and line. A smile curves her lips as she is taken back in time, she can almost feel his arms wrapping her into his like an ivy vine clinging to her for survival. His eyes she can see clearly now, the color of the beautiful-est sky on a summer day.

She imagines herself in his arms again even though she knows to live in the past will only bring her unneeded pain that will once again bring her to her knees in grief. She misses all of their fairy-tale dreams and the nights that they had loved each other with all they could give and feel, remembering the love that had been always so real.

She walks to her closet where a chest still lays; here is where she will find once again all of her memories. Tucked inside is an old brown envelope filled with all of his notes, the sides are now splitting from the years that have gone by, she still sees on it the tears that she has so often cried. She starts to take out the notes he sent as a picture of him falls from her hand, it does not look a day older than when it was sent to her.

She grips it in her hand tightly looking upon his face that she had loved so dearly wondering why their lives had taken the turn that it had so long ago. She looks up at the walls that should carry photos of the family that they had always wished for, by now it should be filled with pictures of their grandchildren as they play in the backyard vigorously searching out their play mates.

A tear falls from her eyes as she takes the last of the letters out of the envelope that has been searched through many times before, to find a letter from war.

Dear Emily it brings me much sadness to write this from afar, your loving fiancé has been buried like so many more have been. He put himself on the line as many times before but this time his soul has found the ending to this forsaking war.

She looks to the walls once again; there are no pictures to see, not even one of her make belief dreams. She closes her eyes and thinks of him as she slowly passes away she sees here is where he has always been waiting. Hand in hand they walk into the light, this is just the beginning of her perfect life.

Have you ever walked outside and the sky is so dark and there is not a star to be found anywhere and the cold bites your skin to the bone and in the next minute your mind awakens and the sky seem so beautiful within the darkness and a warmth runs through you, in that moment you find a peace within yourself that was lost, in that moment you find yourself again and all the pain runs away from you like a waterfall that was dried and forgotten about springing to life again, Flowing its beauty once again to perfection? That is called living through the darkest of times and remembering what life can give you, not what it has taken from you.

The Night's Storm

I sit in the dark thinking of my life and wonder why I feel at such a standstill. I go all day long trying to make the best of it but for some reason I am not even good enough for me, and I wonder why I sit here so lonely.

Dreams leave shadows on my walls of brighter days that never became what I had thought would be a happy ending. I stare at the ceiling trying to figure myself out but am left with too many thoughts and doubt to sort my way through.

I have never felt really at home although I have come very close to it, once upon a time so long ago. I find peace when I hear the water flow or a bird is singing from a tree top wanting to be noticed but yet hiding away in his nest.

The beautiful scenery of fall always takes my breath away; sometimes I wish I could be that bird who never stops his whistling. To be so free must be magical, god I wish I were in that tree singing so beautifully.

It is two in the morning and I have been saying goodnight for hours now, but as always I stare at the four walls that seem to crush me within this confinement that I only wish to escape. I am so tired and my body feels so weak, what I would not give to have one restful night's sleep!

I guess I will blow the candle out once again, stare at the ceiling and walls that holds me in this prison.

The Blaming Game

This year has really been awful; I would like to forget the fact
that most men play the part of a great actor, no heart.

We are going to play the blaming game,
tell me my words are wrong and I will say them again, just the same.

Now I know this group is mostly men
but my words cannot be stopped now that they are written in pen.

Now there are a few that may not be the same,
we have to the right Poet Shi
he writes with a heart that also can feel grief and pain.

To the left we have Santos
all through Facebook you can read his sexy, steamy, lovely poems.

So for now I will play the blaming game,
take my heart from every man!
I don't even wish to feel their hands,
their tears of frustration I can see at a glance,
o yea I know you sir you only want to get into
another girls pants, watch your hands!

I will stay alone as I always have,
post here, post there, post where I can never be found,
never again to feel despair.

I will smile my smile as you talk your denial,
I will take a breath as I push you to your knees;
this girl no longer cares about any man's needs!!!

Hopelessly Awake

I toss and turn as I cry in my sleep,
my body is searching for the one who holds all of me.

I walk through my days as a shadow within myself,
my mind races as it screams out for help.

I am damaged goods at best;
this life I live in has shown me the only peace
I will find is in death.

I speak a million words and still I am never heard,
I cry a thousand tears and yet I am still lingering here.

I pray for release,
all I want is to leave this place that I dread,
this life I have grown to hate,
my being I wish to dissipate,
in my mind this has always been my fate.

A dark shadow can be seen on my wall,
coldness has taken me to hold.
My eyes burn now with no rest,
my heart is pumping frantically inside of my chest.

Sleep is now taking over me
but I will still have to suffer the pain in my dreams.
I will wake in the morning to a new day,
where I will then once again relive all of my pain.

My mind is going insane, I can only find him to blame,
my life never to be the same. I lay down now to play dead;
I wish I could not hear these words that always play on my mind.

I can run but from my mind I can never hide,
the true me for now I will disguise,
my eyes are now burning with despise.
His words were never anything but hopeless lies!

The Bright Side of the Moon

Moonlight shines its brightness on the tree tops
showing us there is as brighter side to the dark
that falls down on us at night.

A night owl screeches his melody from afar
enticing our ears as we search him out,
the moon to show his small shadow, he is quite now.

Peacefulness falls as the moon rises to
its resting place for the night.
The sun is gone but yet it is still so bright
with the endless night sounds of nature's song.

I sit on the porch with a drink in my hand
enjoying the brightness that the night has found.
Peacefulness that you only can found
when the sun once again goes down.

The Dark Side of the Sun

I gaze at the dark side of the sun,
the clouds cover it with the darkness of rain clouds
pouring it's miseries down on us with a vengeance.

I watch the rain
as I reflect on the year that is to be shuffled into my past now
and wonder where the time has went.

I dream of a better year
that will bring me happier memories
to reflect on as the year goes by.

I dream of memories that will fill my heart and mind
with something other than the sound of an old country song,
a love gone wrong.

I pray life gives me more than it has in my past.
The dark side of the sun is now revealed
showing me the brightness that the clouds had
for so long concealed.

Glances

A quick glance over your shoulder,
you used to not be so bold!
His heart you have never forgotten,
with him you felt so at home.

You never grew cold as you lay in his embrace,
the heat from his body to always quicken your blood
leaving behind his gentle love.

A kiss that speaks a thousand words as
he walks out your door once again,
you are left with his undying words of love
as you are made to believe you fit each other like a glove.

A glance over your shoulder once again,
you remember now all of your pain,
he is always to be the same!

A first love to haunt you dreams,
your days are filled with nothing more but his memory.
A taste of his lips is all that you seek,
you could then be lost with nothing more but happy memories.

Poem in a Bottle

I can feel my love drifting closer to me every day.
I walk the sandy shores with a seashell in my hand
as the sand trickles between my toes
tickling me every step of the way.

The moon is almost full
and a purple hue of clouds cover the sky
with the smell of salt lingering in the air.

A wave catches my eyes
and a glass bottle reaches shore, my mind wonders off
thinking of the creatures that live under the sea,
they must feel a surrendering peace,
a killer whale right then yells his grief.

The bottle is now banging on the oceans floor of seashells
that hold it where it is now to lay.
The bottle would of went unnoticed
if I had not walked this far lost in my own thoughts
wondering who would win my heart.

A piece of paper covered in sand
lays in the bottle I now hold in my hand and this is what it reads,
a poem just for me, I now start to read.

I can feel my love getting closer every day.
A girl to call my own on these tiring lonesome days.
A tender hand to hold as I walk down the beach,
no words need to be spoken to build our loving memories.

A kiss to her lips as I bid her goodnight,
her hand softly leaves mine
as I once again wander back into the night.
I can feel my love growing closer every day,
I hear her heart calling out my name.

A poem in a bottle will lead her to me,
or am I to forever be lost in her words of lost memories?

I can feel my love drifting closer to me every day
and until he finds me I will forever sit here and wait.
A poem in a bottle to read every night,
wishing on the stars to give me the man who will
forever be my knight in shining amour.

Hidden Misery

Can you breathe your light into me?
Can you make me see?
Can you make me feel like the person I use to be?

Can you feel my blood as it boils under my skin?
Can you see it running through my veins?
I am full of a bitter sweet pain!

I feel twisted and dark,
my body is being shredded apart.
I fear for my soul,
to many stories yet untold, never to unfold!

I am losing my sanity,
my body no longer wants to breath.
Where is the girl who use to be me?
She is no longer here to be seen!

I walk through life's path,
the one given to me that I shall always carry on my back.
I look for the sun,
I am only blinded by the dark, my mind had been torn apart.

I fall asleep; I look for me, the girl that use to be!
Hidden misery is all that I can see, no longer am I me!

Past Tremors

Reliving dark memories that were hidden for so long,
my mind has lost its will to fight the terrors off.

I can remember them like it was yesterday;
my mind is to forever remember
what was lost so long ago.

Night sweats and tremors run through my body,
I am so tired and weak I cannot even think
of anything else but the fatigue that I feel.

I find myself looking off into space
not seeing the life around me that I want to live.
I only see my past!

The one I want to forget and put behind me,
why is that all I can see?

Fighting Gloves

He is cruel, he is dark,
he laughs at my broken heart.
He left me torn and shattered apart,
he walks away with my once loving heart.

His words will never be the same.
his dreams of us to go up into a burning flame.
My life is to always be a blaming game of pain.

He is no better than the devils spawn,
he was not raised to be the man he is today,
his heart can no longer be seen or found,
it lays on the ground.

He finds his excuses and tells them so readily,
he believes they are true and should be believed.
His lies are now seen
he is nothing more than a deceiver.

He deserves nothing more in this life but hurt and grief!
He ruined the girl that once was,
she hides in a corner with her fighting gloves ready and armed,
making sure her heart never again will be harmed.

I am going to take this one step at a time,
I am going to show him once again my heart will be mine.
He believes I will never be the same;
he wants to leave me torn and shaken.

I will show him the girl that once was,
can once again take off her fighting gloves.
I will show him what he lost when he decided
my heart could easily be tossed.

Numb

I am searching for me but I am numb
and only see you as your face flashes behind my eyes,
I can still see you as you hide behind your disguise.

I have come un-done as I try to see my heart
I am faced with the fears that I have always found,
once again I feel numb.

I drown in my own tears as I scream out your name,
my body feels needless pain and here I go again,
darkness hides me as I protect myself from my fears and pain.

You never knew me at all, I never knew you at all!
You hide behind a cloak, words misspoken.
Take my heart with you as you go it can be the devils token.

Take my soul and let it go into my own made hell,
I have given up never again to rebel!
Never to feel, nothing has ever been real!

You are the devils warrior taking all that you can,
next time you run for cover you will find no peace by my hand!
I am black, I am cold, I am the person you let unfold.

I will try to wake up one day but for now
in my darkness is where I feel safe!
Wake me up when the light can be seen again;
wake me up when life has more to share than pain.

Defend or Bend

I have to take it slow,
my heart has been used to many times
to just be thrown out into the cold.

I relive demons just when I try to restart my life,
always to throw me back into the darkness that I try to hide.

I have to search for me before I let another in,
this is the way my life has always been.
My life is not one I want to rush,
I cannot be pushed into a corner
or I will hide once again to never be seen.

I will linger here for as long as I need,
live my life searching for my own dreams.

I am not cruel,
I have not always been so dark,
this is just what the men in my life have taught me.

I am always on alert,
always ready to defend my heart until the end.

Failed Test

Frighteningly surreal the way that my heart
has fended off anyone that can hurt me
but yet anyone that also could fix me.

I am to keep myself hidden
away in this place of perplexed hiding,
this is where no one can find me.

Cower of a day and hide of a night,
this world no longer one I want to fight;
it is to give me nothing but spite.

I was put here to be hurt by another's hand,
my life has shown me I am no more than a toy
for the pleasures of man.

I sit with a cloak covering my eyes,
for now on I will not be recognized.
I have been penalized for trusting again,
once more my heart to defend!

I will give no more, I will receive much less,
this is what my heart has come to realize.
I have always failed the test!

Untitled?

Have you ever walked outside and the sky is so dark
and there is not a star to be found anywhere
and the cold bites your skin to the bone
and in the next minute your mind awakens
and the sky seems so beautiful within the darkness
and a warmth runs through you,
in that moment you find a peace within yourself that was lost,
in that moment you find yourself again
and all the pain runs away from you like a waterfall
that was dried and forgotten about springing to life again,
Flowing its beauty once again to perfection?
That is called living through the darkest of times
and remembering what life can give you,
not what it has taken from you.

Don't

Don't look at me with your conniving eyes,
I can see you hiding behind your disguise, your walls of lies.

Don't ask me to trust you,
any love I have ever felt for you has turned to dust,
like a tin can on a shelf turning to rust.

Don't beg for my forgiveness,
you do not deserve to rest easily
after all of your heartless deceiving.

Don't tell me you are sorry,
you never meant for any of this to happen!
Twice now you have walked out of my door believing
I will be here when you need me, just again to deceive me!

Don't think I will play anymore of your games,
I have finally learned that you
will only again cause me unneeded pain.

Don't think of me when you are alone and tired,
my memory will only to you be one of lust and desire.
My memory of you is one that burns
in hell's fringing fire, a hate like no other.

Don't look at me searching for the once sweet angel;
she has left this place,
leaving you in your own man made disgrace.

Coming Out of the Dark

You can only be blind for so long before you see
the light that was shining in front of you from the beginning.

The song can play over and over in your head,
in the end you will finally understand the meaning to the words
that lays behind the beautiful melody.

Your memories can haunt you when you sleep,
your days can be filled with the answers you so badly want to seek.
In the end you will be left with nothing but unanswered questions.

You can fight the demons that hide in your heart,
but in the end you will finally see the light
that had always kept you in the dark.

Your life when you are ready will always restart
and your dreams will once again be all you search for,
they are the only thing that is worth your fight.

Finally to See

Broken heart, restless mind,
you blame me for all of your lies.

Shedding tears,
two years believing your heart was really here,
you were just a figment of my imagination.

Best friends until the end,
never did I believe you would turn out worse than him.

Blazing pain beats in my chest, my heart will never feel again,
never again to be stupid enough to trust.

Traumatized from the hurt you found so easily to give me,
you sit and laugh because I believed in the man that you let on to be.

I believed you were like no other, you had the perfect heart
and in your arms I always felt rediscovered.

You tricked me twice,
you ruined my life and now you believe
I have no reason to feel deceived,
hurt and no longer trusting.

You were a figment of my imagination,
you were never as you perceived to be,
in my arms you were just playing with me.

Left with a broken heart, dreams that are now torn apart.
Now I can finally see, no man deserves all of me.

Endless mazes
I sit here and I wonder and wish I knew
why your words were nothing more than broken lies.

I believe that we all have an angel that will help us along the way,
someone to help us find our way through life's endless mazes.

I trusted and I believed every word
that you had ever told me.
I believed we were meant to be
and had to fight our way to finally see.

You told me of your heart and dreams
and of everything she could never give to thee.
Here I sit alone wondering why you were so full of lies
and why your heart was always one under disguise.

I never would have believed you were only a man
who wanted to use me as you deceived me.
I gave up everything I had worked so hard for,
just to be your whore!

You tell me over and over this is not so,
that your heart was true.
How can I believe anything you say when you sit there
letting her pay, for anything you wish for?
I guess she then would be your money whore.

Can you talk to her about your dreams and past things?
I know you cannot because with her you can never trust!
You tell me that this is not what you wished;
you were confused until she left!

Can we be honest as we were for so long?
Like a country song,
you cannot trust her with your all
and to think so you will only take a heartbreaking fall.

I have learned by your words only that she has only her heart
and family at mind, tell me I am wrong
and that you have never said this much is true, your heart you will
always have to hide from the one who never really knew you.

Take your steps into the dark,
follow her dreams that you have never wanted.
Let her belittle you and your family because that
is really what you dream, things.

Kill the one who knows you through and through,
never to give real thought of your loss.
One day you will see that
I would have been the only one to fulfill your dreams!

She hears his thoughts from far away;
his hearts desires he cannot keep at bay.
His dreams of finding the right one always on his mind,
someone that even he cannot define or even dream to ever find.

He looks into the sparkling fire alone in his own thoughts,
wishing his nights were spent in the arms of the perfect one for him.
Dreams of her as he drifts off to sleep,
in the morning he is left with only her memory.

False Integrity

Look out the window, what do you see?
Forbidden memories of the one
who has done nothing more than to deceive.

Integrity must not have been his thing,
that would make him be what he always wanted me to see.

Look at your shadow, what do you see?
Only one because you are alone as you have always been.

The truth would of set me free,
if he had not felt like I was nothing more than unfeeling.

I am not the innocent believing girl
you found here waiting for someone to really care,
she left when your lies told her
you really were never here.

Look at me what do you see?
A girl who no longer believes
in the lies you have always told me,
no longer am I that easy to deceive!

Childhood Dreams

Childhood dreams turned to dust, as I walk down these halls
I search to see a picture hanging on the walls of me.

I bunk in a room with friends I have grown to love,
we all wish for a happy home.
A birthday party and sleep over to,
a mother and father to hear say I love you.

Wishing to have what others do, playing a game of baseball or two.
Arms to hold me when I have a nightmare,
a kiss to my cheek to remind me my family is near.

A hopeless dream of a better life,
wishing for so much more as I wake up to the same lonely sight.
Another child cries in his sleep,
he reminds me of my own terrifying dreams.

I buckle down on my knee once more
and pray for the same things I did the night before.
A happy home is all I want and a family just to call my own.

I may never get my childhood dreams,
I may never walk down a hall to see a picture of me,
but I can dream of a family and pretend they are near;
sometimes this dries my downpouring tears.

Heart of Steel

I have torn the picture that was my guidance
with every step I took and every breath that I breathed.

The shirt I wore to find you in my dreams
is now made of ash in a pit, no longer to be seen.
The color blue to match your eyes is now
as dark as the midnight sky.

I have made my heart cold as ice when I think of you
and all of your alibis,
demanding dreams you wished from me,
you thought you took everything or so it seems.

I have grown to be a stronger person,
my mind and dreams will no longer get away from me.
I have grown smarter along the way,
no longer will a man use me for play.

I sometimes wish for the girl who use to be me
to come back from deep in beneath
but she is lost and hiding never to trust again,
never to feel any pain.

I walk through my day now with a smile on my face
and look at you as nothing more than a disgrace.
My love was true and you were not,
leaving behind a girl in the dark.

I am stronger than you have ever been and
you will one day suffer this same pain,
in my heart you are now left out,
no more will I let you bring me down.

Roads to Travel

Everything is finally starting to come together,
the life I dreaded so much has an open door now
to fulfillment and completion of dreams.

I never thought the day would come when
I could finally have a smile on my face
that reached my mind and heart
all together in total anticipation.

I know it is going to be a long road ahead of me
but the trail is not hidden by fallen branches
and debris that hide what lays on the other side any longer,
giving me open space to walk freely.

I have fought many battles in my life
to come out on top in most of them,
only some I lost but a winner in the end.

I have had many unrealistic dreams I thought
but now I see it was just a matter of waiting, pursuing,
and never giving up on what I want the most,
my dreams to come true.

I will fight any battle handed to me from here on out
knowing they may never come about
but always staying true to myself and never giving up.

A Fight for a Fighter

I am trying to think of the words to say,
to ease just some of your pain.

A fighter who gave his all, fighting for what he believed was right,
never to take a fall while he fought for us all.

His time had come where he could once again
enjoy the freedom he helped give us all,
this was a freedom that would not last long.

We write on each other's walls
replying to statuses that really mean nothing at all
never to give a second thought to a soldiers fall.

Let's take the time to read his story and sign a little block,
lets show him we appreciated the time he took from his life,
to fight a war to keep us safe and letting us see the morning light.

Forgotten I Love Yous

I still think of you
even though I beg my mind to forget the man
who always seemed to make me blue, always to be untrue.

I still dream of our dreams that we spent night after night
planning to fulfill, never to realize you
never had a real heart to feel.

I still cry myself to sleep in the dead of night,
my heart now bares a hole that you left behind.
My tears never to dry!

I still giggle when I remember the way you would smile at me,
so easy to see the mischief behind your eyes, a secret surprise.

My heart still warms when I remember the I love yous,
always so sweet when coming from you,
I wish they had been true! Because I will always love you.

I still have my crying fits when I think of everything you did,
the hurt still lingers in my heart,
that I have tried to turn dark.

A glimmer of light to shine through every time
I remember the fake you.
Wishing I had never meant the one who had hurt me,
the one I can seem to never forget.

I don't write because I am bored or lonely,
I have tons that I could be doing
and kids that love to make me messes!

I write because that is the only times I can be honest
with the feelings I would rather hold in my heart
and never let escape my mind,
I write to give myself relief from life...

Last Stance

I have slept my day away, thinking of all the lies
it was so easy for you to say, my heart to play.

I have had dreams that torture me,
hating myself for all the time I was to blind to see.
You were not the man you perceived!

I am kind of glad you did what you did,
now I can see the real man that you hid. I will never forgive!

You believed in the one who has always deceived,
always to make me prove it her and not me.
No longer will I waste my time, making you see all of her lies.

One day you will wake up from the cold
and in that moment all of her lies will finally unfold.
As always to leave you empty, cold and ready to fold.

One day you will remember how to feel,
knowing you lost the only one who ever cared
about the heart you use to reveal.

I have loved you my whole life through,
never to fake my love for you.
Not many have given you that chance,
to be yourself no matter what kind of man.

In my mind I can finally see,
the hurt and torment you wanted for me.
In my heart I can still not believe,
you are the man you now have perceived to me.

I loved you with a heart that was true
she has never loved you for you.

I will take that away with me knowing now
you will live nothing short but a life full of lies and misery,
that you will always believe.

The Monster That Lies Beneath

The monster is gone he now is to be believed that he sleeps,
never to realize he is wide awake,
because the girl he no longer has to hide as he fakes his days...

Once she is gone though he will then really sleep,
to be woken with just one word to be spoken,
a song that plays, reminding him of other days...

He will hunt her down,
look for her all around because even his own words
admit another like her can never again be found...

He wants to believe he no longer needs the one
who in his heart can always see.
His mind to read, hers just the same,
the only one who can feel his true pain...

Put her away on a shelf so high,
but to be warned the monster is not asleep in hiding,
she is just close enough now for him to find...

Seeking Memories

I cannot stop pacing;
my mind is racing thinking of days
that I felt like my life was in a better place.

I walk out onto my porch and see the sky so lit up,
beautiful colors of pinks and purples can be seen
behind the now leafless trees.

I wonder is there really life beyond what the naked eye can see
a life that can be lived for all of eternity.

Can your dreams really be found or is it just words that keep
your soul lifted off of the ground?

Lights can be seen glimmering from other houses
and I cannot help but wonder
is their lives all that they dreamt of and sought out.

I am told over and over to move on with my life
but I cannot stop thinking of the one,
who seemed so right,
his memories always controlling my life.

At moments like this I just want to forget
what my life has always seemed to give!
I want to dream big and laugh loud,
forget about everyone who has ever hurt my heart,
I want to leave that part of my life in the dark, restart!

Starting a new life seems so right at this moment
but there is so many things I cannot forget about and leave behind.

When I close my eyes at night I know I am bound to find
the dreams I use to wish for, my eyes are always to open those doors.

He is always to be found to me, in my dreams
I always seek out to find my memories,
of the love that has been lost to me.

Sparks

A spark has lit my mind,
I wonder what you would do if I was no longer here to find.

Your every word to be hidden forever because the one
who has always been here to listen will no longer
be here to discover, gone away from you forever.

Your every dream and fantasy to go unfinished,
left in your mind to fester, simmer, left for another to blemish.

The hardest thing that I will ever have to do
is say bye to the one in a kind you.

When you sit in that darkened room,
things on your mind that you need to let loose
you will then think of the one who was always there,
the one who let you be you!
Where you always felt safe enough to
share the dreams you will always bare.

Kids at Play

It's so gloomy outside I say to the kids,
you have to just stay in and pout!!

But mom we have played in worse,
this is just you being mean of course.

It's raining and thundering!
Don't you see the lightning flashing?
It will strike you down to the ground.

Mom you just don't understand us at all,
we just want to go outside and play ball.

We are bored and you keep us trapped, we get so tired of that!
If you had ever been young before you would let us past this door!

We are bored don't you see? We just want to go outside and play!

Can you please let us be free?
We promise when we come back in
you will not hear one more complaint from her or me.

So I say this to my little children,
if you are bored I can find you something to do!
Go wash a dish or two!

The floors need vacuumed, the trash needs taken out,
get your lips out of that pout!

Then there is always your room and homework to!
I can find plenty for you to do!

O mom they exclaim, we forgot there is an inside game we can play,
we will help you do chores on another day!

As they scamper to their rooms, I laugh and say
don't forget the broom and clean your bedrooms!!

Lost Dreams

I was never given the chance to show him who I really am,
he only seen the little part that I allowed him in.

Always shy to give my all but for him
I came closer than I had ever been, now to remember
why I kept a part of me to always be hidden.

I have many dreams that I have never told
now to forever be enclosed and left in the cold,
I never could tell it all because in my mind
I knew I would fall.

If he had just given me a fighting chance
he would of finally seen what real love was all about.
He will never find the same thing, not with her or anybody.

He has never had what I wanted to give a love
that runs deep into my veins. My heart is forever to be broken
and never from my lips could those words ever again be spoken.

I am to live a very lonely life, sitting here alone in the dark,
never again will I dream of anything other than a life
of coldness that has set into my heart.

A Poet's Heart

I am putting it down even if I have to use crayon,
it does not matter where I am or who is around.

I am a poet and I write the words that haunt my heart
day in and day out and sometimes you may even get a glimpse
of what I am really about.

I say things that may hurt your heartstrings or even
make you smile when your life seems to be
at the end of the road with no hope.

I put myself in all that I say, my fingertips says it all
when my mouth could never tell you my real thoughts.

I sit in a room all to myself writing my feelings down
for all to read and just hope that someday my words
will give you what you need to feel,
to give your life more meaning and more
than anything a chance to heal.

Heart Pains

I would be lying if I said your love is not the one
I always wished to find,
and now that it is gone my life has left me cold and blind.

Memories flood back to me of times we felt so free,
in your loving arms I knew
I did not have to be anything other than the real me.

I still dream of the things we were meant to be
and all of the things we were always excited about
and wanted to see, torturing memories.

I have heart pains that won't go away, they leave me restless,
tired and so very dreary. My heart has been broken
in a thousand little pieces and my mind won't let me be at peace.

I ask myself so many times in the day
what could I of done to make him truly love me
and only me, my pain will never really be seen
my heart wanting to take its last beat.

My pillow to stay soaked in the tears that I cry,
all I want is the answer to why
it is always my heart that is to be denied.
My pain never means anything at all
and I am always the one to take the heartbreak fall.

I will sit here and wonder these things all through my days,
looking out the window the season will never change,
I will always feel this unbearable pain, my heart never to feel again.

I will sit here by candle lights always to wonder
what I had not done right
to be the one to see your beautiful face
in the mornings light.

Petals

The last petal has long ago fell from the rose,
the leaves that were so colorful
now have fallen to the ground from the trees.

A light cover of ice to the grass
that just a month ago was so flush and full,
now dying as it waits for new.

Crisp air to hit you in your face
as you walk into a cold winter's night.
The stars always seem to sparkle
a brighter light on these winter nights.

Christmas decorations are glowing all around,
children excited to know it is once again Santa time.

A snow flurry can be seen in the air,
melting as soon as it hits the ground leaving it so bare.

Waiting for winter's wonderland to be seen,
beautifully covered white trees is what I please.

Misplaced Feelings

I guess you know this is me again
writing once again my words of pain.
I done what I knew was wrong to do in my heart,
trusting the devils words again never to believe
he once again wanted to deceive me
and throw me in the dark.

I believed he had finally seen what he truly means to me.
He came back like a gust of wind,
saying words of love and our future was now to begin.
I put my whole self and trust into it again as I had before,
just to be once again knocked down on to the floor.
The promises of heartache finally coming to an end
should of been in a love song written.

I sit here as I always have,
crying my tears that had just barely dried.
I keep asking the same question as I had before,
how can you say you love me just too once again
leave me tormented and torn.

Life had seemed like it was finally going to fit into place,
once again you have shown me I was nothing more but a disgrace,
my love and trust once again misplaced.

Given

I can take no more, my life has beat me
until I now know I need to give in.

So many things that have been my life,
showing me happiness would never be found,
I now have to end the fight.

My mind has taken all it can, my heart to never mend.
I have unbearable pain, my life to put me in my grave.

My dreams will never come true,
I was just never strong enough to come through,
never good enough it seemed to.

I feel the pain surging through my body,
I sit alone with nobody.
Waiting for it to be said and done,
no longer strong enough to fight a life
that has never been right.

I will love you no matter what,
but I think my body is finally ready to give up.
If it is time I want you to know
I will be watching you know matter where I go.

A truer love I could never have felt,
even though you deny and hide it from us...

Dare to Live

Trusting and daring
my heart that has always been conspiring against me.

Hurting and thinking that my dreams won't die without he,
I am set out to make them more than fantasies.

Dreams will come true with the one who seeks them out
wanting to share them to.

Burning heart, blustering cold,
no one will make me die without great stories to be told.

I am going to live the life that I seek,
be myself and never live in hiding because I love myself
and there is no one that can deny me...

A Sister's Love

A love to fly away lead by an angel in waiting,
leaving behind a family full of pain.

A friendship like no other,
a sisters love that will never be forgotten.

Stories now to be remembered of laughter and younger days
where life was nothing more but dreams to be discovered.

Tears now fall in her absence
but her memories will never be forgotten and every day
with her you will always love and cherish.

A heart so full of love
for her family and friends has been seen from above,
the lord had now taken her hand,
into the heavens where her body can mend.

A sadness to creep back into your heart,
crying for the days you now have to spend apart.

You look up at the sky and it seems so dark,
just at that moment you see a flashing star,
calmness takes a hold of you, knowing it is her saying
here is where I will be waiting and watching over you.

Trust to Dust

I have writers block,
in my mind the words are there
but in my heart they stay hidden and scared.

I have dreams that I can easily write
but in my mind I know to chase them
would be nothing more than an endless fight.

I have memories that remind me of a love so true
but in my mind I now know
he was only a figment of my imagination too.

I have tears that cannot understand
why the man of my dreams has left me torn
and shaking with despair and fear.

I will never again be able to trust,
in my mind his deceit will linger and rust.
Leaving me cold, my heart turning to dust!

Dreams of Her

A strangers words, beautifully written,
the things that come from his heart
is never to be hidden.

A word of love, and the dreams he wishes for,
waiting for the perfect one to walk through his hearts door.

A memory that leaves him saddened,
for the words he wished he had said,
now to stay on his mind to tread.

A candle lit, music to play low,
loving the thoughts his mind is always to bestow.
A loving heart he wants to share and show!

Waiting for the day to come when
he can share his thoughts and heart
with the one he is to grow old with.

A Liar's Game

I have done it again,
let the same man show me pain.
What have I ever done that was not right?
To make his heart for me
always be nothing more than ice.

I trusted him as I had before,
he once again told me I was nothing to him
but his here and there whore.

I have always done as I was told,
believing him even when his heart
I should of remembered is shut off and cold.

He deserves a life of hell,
for the way he treats the ones who care.
Never believe a man like he, they can make you believe
and then leave you like trash in the street.

The Seekers

Never did I think this would be me,
once again to be used just to make another man happy.

A life full of hurt,
tears that have never ever really mattered.
My heart to always be left tattered.

A whole life never to feel right,
from a child men have
used me to make their bodies feel right.

I am left to never trust again,
the words that I hear in a love song.
The one who promised so much
only wanted me again to touch.

He swore he loved me so,
just to once again make me cry and leave me alone.
I should have known,
I am just a whore that will never feel at home.

I will from here on out
let any man do as he pleases, his lies of love
I will never again believe.

I am nothing more but a whore to be played
I learned this from a striking young age.
I am worth nothing and will always be,
just the girl men seek out so they can be pleased.

Died of a Broken Heart

She sets heart broken, regretting the chance she had taken. Her life to be full of heartaches and fights, even her childhood was never right. She held it all in, tucked away kept her safe. She endured a life of pain and promised to herself she would never trust again. He walked into her life making her trust, breaking down walls that were built. Making dreams that was never to be, promising her the moon through his dreams. Walking out the way that he came, no regards to her suffering pain she laid in her bed starved herself until she lost half of her weight. Crying for all he promised, her heart she should never have trusted.

Into her life he came again, promising this time she would not find that pain again. Fulfilling a dream his wished, now out as he treats her once again like trash, walking away as he laughs. She sets and waits for the devil to take her away; starving herself so she once again does not have to endure the same pain. She is strong now in a different way, she no longer has a heart that feels the same. She sits and cries wondering why, he lied again just to in the end after he got what he wanted to say goodbye.

She wonders how he could be so cruel, she always believed his heart was true, always to say he only done what he felt he had to do. She will set and wait for the time to come, living the rest of her life in hell. She will die of a broken heart, the one he believed he had a right to tear apart. Her tears cannot stop now, she had never been good enough for anyone, and they hurt her just for their pleasurable fun. She will go to hell in the end she knows this well, but her life had already been one to live in hell. She will die of a broken heart; he then can laugh at the girl he shredded apart.

Never to be the Same

In his mind I will always stay,
no matter what words you want to believe!
I have it written right in front of me.

His words of once again searching for me
but this to has to stay in secret, tired of it!

His mind you will never have, he told me that could never be,
I never lie, I have everything I need
to back up the words I say to thee.

A cold heart I now have,
sometimes I think and know that is bad,
but I have learned from the best
and the old me has left this place full of deceit.

I once had a heart of gold,
loving all who needed a friend,
I was there never on the defend.
My mind screams for the old me,
but he took that with him.

Phantom

A phantom in the dark, seeking your heart,
in the end he will tear it apart.

He will grab your soul right from your chest, at best
you will get a half of it back.

He will make you believe you are a part of his dreams,
he will tell you he loves you
and ask why can you not trust me.

He will shatter the walls you have worked so hard to build,
your feelings and heart you will spill.

He will then after all of this is done,
take what part of you is left and run.

He is the phantom of your days,
the one who can hurt you in every way, while he plays.

He is the phantom of your dreams,
the one who once made you always believe.
Even when you were always scared to once again be deceived.

He is the man of your dreams,
the one who takes your soul and heart
as he once again leaves, crushed miserably!

Blissfully Perfect

A weekend full of happy memories,
wondering if now it was only trickery.

Jokes to be told, each other to hold. Hurts to be told,
with the only one your trust can be held.

Fears of life that you cannot hide,
being told in words that only we can describe.

Bodies finding the one that they missed,
soft and passionate kisses.
Bodies in bliss!

I never want to leave this place,
always loving to see his face.

First Moves

Hearts broken with the words never spoken.

Tears of frustrations to pour,
needing more.

Complicated series of events need to vent.

Begging for truths, that can only come from you.
Wanting and waiting for dreams to come true.
I cannot make the first move, until I know what I am to you.

Scared to put myself out there,
if my heart is to suffer once again in despair.

Waiting to hear the words you had once spoken,
my breath I keep holding.

Needing to feel more,
cannot live my life any longer
not knowing what you feel.

Night Sounds

The nights wonder all around,
where a beautiful moon is to be found.

Crickets sing into the night,
an owl can be heard from the trees height.

Deer settle down for the night,
making a bed in the brush to hide.

A snort can be heard in the dark,
a lone deer in search of his lover.

A peaceful calm takes hold of me,
loving the feel of the nights air
and the sounds that can only be found right here.

Perfectly Incorrect

Perfectly incorrect you always are,
I also hold the heart.

Conniving everyone says,
maybe you taught him his ways.

Believe what you want, believe what you say,
I know you are once again wrong today.

Never to have listened to the words he had in his heart,
never to understand more than your part.

Always blaming everyone for the mistakes made,
knowing you made just as many.

I have had my share of the words you say,
even though I know they are more lies to be said.

Never were you there to see the man who really stood there.
Never a real heart would you share.

Do as you want I really don't care,
the words you say does not still linger here.

In his words I will trust, we were made for each other,
we both have real hearts.

Never will I need to learn how to love him more,
once again he has proven I am not his mere plaything!

Undying Love

An undying love that is like no other,
a love of my life to discover.

Happy chills surround my heart,
never could I love another.

Dreams at night to wake me and remember,
nightmares gone as I slumber.

Never to believe I could be this happy,
never to believe this could be me.

My prayers have finally been answered,
my life no longer one of despair.

My soul is to take a new height,
in the arms of a love that feels so right.

Never to wish for anything more,
the perfect person has taken me away,
loving him until my dying day...

A Soldier's Pride

They have weathered the storm
leaving their homes with nothing more
than a bag to pack on their made to be toughened backs.

A glance one last time at the family
they are to leave behind,
a tear to leave their eyes wondering
if this would be their last goodbye.
A pride like no other consumes their bodies,
to fight for what they believe is right, never to hide.

Standing proud at the services that they will have to join,
fallen friends and other memorable boys.
A little more their hearts will have to bare,
to not see the brother in arms
that at one time stood beside them holding no fear.

Coming home to a world they no longer know,
seeing that all of their blood
and tears have for so many others given endless hope.

Their shoulders back as they walk another step,
feeling a pride that most will never have,
never did they hide and never will they forget
the friends that were lost and the blood that was spilled.

A Life So Divine

With every breath I take
and every beat of my heart
I wish nothing more for my splendid life.
Perfect by far!

With every sunset that touches my eyes,
nothing more could I find.
A beautiful life so divine,
a beautifier life could never be defined.

My smiles to reach the stars above,
they are higher than the moon I so love
. A shooting star to fall from the sky,
no more wishes to find.

A happiness to take over me,
no more tears do I cry
as I drift off to sleep.

Awaken to a perfect sunrise,
one that looks like
it was made just for me and my eyes.

A tear to leave my eyes,
fullness I cannot describe,
my heart could of never been so surprised.

It shines brighter than the sun ever could've.
To truly feel love!

Wondrous Dreams

A beauty in the night's sky,
how I have missed so much,
covered by the tears I so often cried.

The sun to shine in my eyes,
telling me to once again enjoy and live life.
You are not alone any longer, in your dreams you belong.

A song to softly play,
a melody that puts your heart at ease.

A bird to flutter by,
its wings spread far and wide.
Enjoying this perfect high.

Lay down and fall into a peaceful sleep,
wondering if I am just living a wondrous dream.
Wake up to a new day, happy to be in this place.

Your Words, My Life

Dear Lord tell me where I shall be,
my heart has for so long lingered in misery.

You tell us to pray for better things,
hearts to love you for always.

My life has not been one of your happily writings,
no matter what I do it seems.

I can do no right,
I can do no wrong, confused it seems
when hearing your loving songs.

I pray a million things!
Of my heart and soul, what means the most to me,
You cannot see!

To be a hypocrite is not me,
to walk through your doors would be a fake,
that step I cannot make.

I believe in the words you write
I believe my heart with you would always be right.

My heart cries out for the unseen,
a man I have forever held in my dreams.

Give me this one thing that I will always breathe,
and then maybe your book is one I will forever believe.

Truly Yours

Your arms are the only place I want to stay,
hearing the words you have to say.

I never felt so loved before,
to search for anything else no more.

I cannot deal with anymore heartache,
your words are the only thing I want to believe.

Back to take my heart away,
lingering where it has always and forever stayed.

No one can take my happiness away,
no words other than yours can I believe.

My heart cries out for you, with all that you say and do.
I sit here to wait for you, my love always to be true.

Resting Hearts

Hearts to rest when they feel their best,
loving life with no regrets.

Living in sunshine no matter how cold outside,
it's a feeling I cannot describe.

A smile on my face, that once had lost its place.
Thinking it would forever be erased.

Perfectly surrendering in such a sweet place,
feelings I hope to never escape.

My heart could never be happier, my life never so full.
A love that is to always follow through.

My soul to take a new height,
to splendidly fly into the heavens night.

A day to remember, in arms I splendor.

Caresses

Caress me gently,
show me the way a body should feel, chills!

Whisper endearing words into my ears,
pleasing me into tears.

Bolts of lightning going through my body,
to feel like somebody.

My heart to explode with passionate love,
what dreams are made of.

Caress me once, caress me twice,
caress my body as you entice.

Take me to unknown heights,
feeling you all night feels so right.

Pull me as close as you can,
love me until night's end.

Shuddering Memories

I woke with a start this morning,
coldness hits my face reminding me of a long ago place.

Shimmers of lost memories can be remembered
as I shudder in all too well known surrender.

My heart starts to pound out of control,
my body shakes with the chillness it still holds.

My mind takes a new turn,
slowly my body starts to warm.

The shaking goes away,
as I remember I am now safe.

I start the day,
with positive things to say.

A smile on my face,
as I leave this place.

Sweet Perfection

Life getting better over time my heart once again to shine.
My eyes sparkling with diamonds!

My laughter and happiness can be heard miles always,
just from the smile on my face.

Stories to be told, laughter and tears to flow,
some memories are of happier times
while others are from a sadness that keeps you so very cold,
either way needs to be told.

Connections to share, no words to be spared.
A trust like no other, I can tell of everything
in my life that has brought me despair
that so easily you can uncover.

Always to be here for the one who knows me best,
knowing in me his words he can also entrust.
Secrets to never be, souls to truly see.

Like a kettle on a low fire, to simmer to perfection.
A soul to find such a sweet connection,
trusting only one with everything.
A tear to leave my eyes, with you I can never hide.

EXCLUSIVE PREVIEW

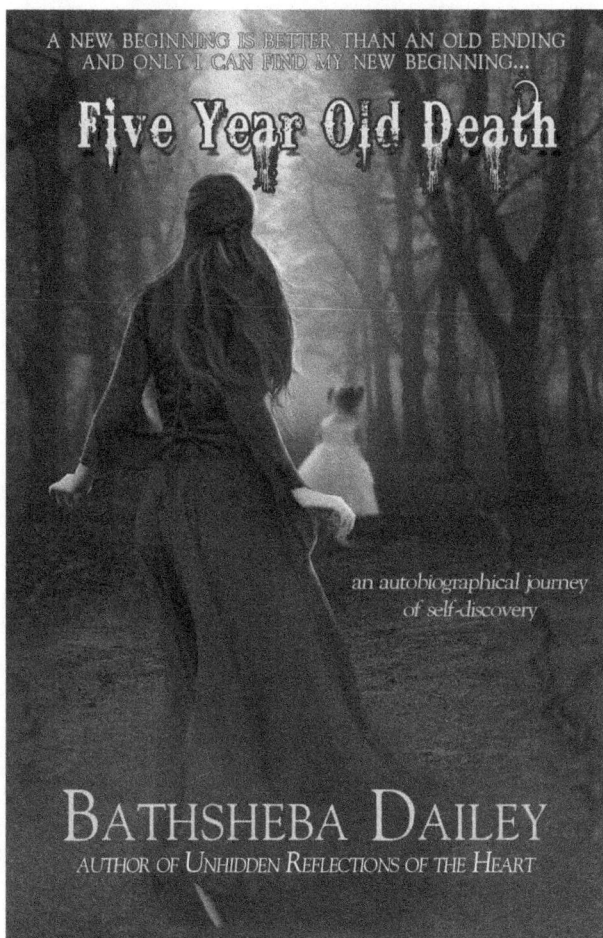

A NEW BEGINNING IS BETTER THAN AN OLD ENDING
AND ONLY I CAN FIND MY NEW BEGINNING...

Five Year Old Death

an autobiographical journey
of self-discovery

BATHSHEBA DAILEY
AUTHOR OF UNHIDDEN REFLECTIONS OF THE HEART

A HEARTFELT MEMOIR AND
AUTOBIOGRAPHY NOW
AVAILABLE IN PRINT
AND EBOOK

ONE

FIVE YEAR DEATH

I t is what I see in my nights of restless sleep that torment me in my waking hours. I search for what I will never find and find what will only drive me into hell a little deeper every day. I have always been just me and that has been fine and I love the heart that I have been blessed with even through a life that I could take or leave without any turns looking back. Does this mean I do not love my family or children? Does this mean that I really want to die in my sleep like I beg every night before I once again fall into my own hell of night tremors? This is something I ask myself every single breathing day that I am made to exist on earth! I love my children but maybe just maybe they would be better off without a mother who cries in her sleep for no reason that they could ever understand or that I would even want to tell them. I am alone in the crowded room that everyone talks about and that may be okay for some but I was meant to love and cherish those who walk in my life. I am lost in the dark and followed by the shadows that are to forever haunt me with nowhere to run but back within myself. I cry a million unseen tears that I hide with a pretty smile upon my face that I wish to let run free and to be seen by just one person that will maybe understand me and understand what I am forever left to feel. I am not mentally ill by any chemical imbalance!

I am however mentally ill by the life that I have been given and at the end of the day after I have tried to make everyone else's life pretty with a pink ribbon, I am left to wonder;

"Did they see me?"

I want the fairytale romance that will never come into my life for it has already been here, but once again it left me driving down the road on four wheels taking any dreams I may have had with him. I want to sit in a rocking chair and not say one word to my mate but yet hear a thousand stories through his heartbeat. I search for that person that you never have to see but yet you can read him with just the silence of his nothing. I search for what we had with each other and I am left to wonder how he could so easily let that go like we were nothing more but a raincloud that would be okay once it poured its life upon the world. So many things I am left to wonder about as the tears run swiftly down my cheeks, so many things that I wish to escape beginning with me. I am left here with nothing more than a life full of grief that has been handed down to me since I was five years old in age. I am living in the tormented mind and soul of a five year olds death! Before you read any farther I will be blunt, if you are looking for a book of perfection and cover ups in feelings then this is not the book for you. I am writing of my life that only I have lived and no one can dictate or change a word of what I feel and think is the reason I carry depression on the sleeve of a lost soul just waiting to be found and understood. I am writing of a past worth forgetting that haunts me every day of my life! I am writing the story that only I can tell!

EXPERIENCE THE POETRY OF

BATHSHEBA DAILEY

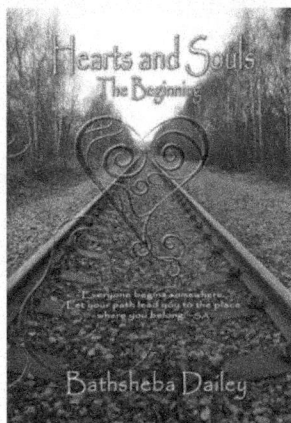

ALL TITLES AVAILABLE ON
AMAZON IN PRINT & EBOOK

About the Poetess

Writing has become something that Bathsheba Dailey has to do to continue on through her life. She finds peace within her words and a better understanding of who she is and who she wants to be remembered as.

She lives in a small town in West Virginia with her three young girls and has completed her associate's degree in business management. She strides to make a better life for her loved ones no matter the cost to herself. As always, a new beginning is better than an old ending.

Social Media & Web Links

FACEBOOK PROFILE
www.facebook.com/bathshebadailey

FACEBOOK PAGES
www.facebook.com/AuthorBathshebaDailey
www.facebook.com/FiveYearOldDeath

BLOG
www.beth-frommyheart.blogspot.com

WEBSITE
www.bathshebadailey.com

TWITTER
www.twitter.com/Bathsheba15

GOOGLE +
www.plus.google.com/u/0/101184968789960146323/posts

Meet the Designers

Cover design, interior book design,
and eBook design
by Blue Harvest Creative
www.blueharvestcreative.com

www.ingramcontent.com/pod-product-compliance
Lightning Source LLC
Chambersburg PA
CBHW021200020426
42331CB00003B/150